This book is dedicated to the young readers in my life:
Cole, Jayden, Holly, & Charlotte

Keep reading it will only make you stronger!

The dialects used in this book are Swampy Cree and Manitoba Ojibway/Saulteaux

bear

makwa

maskwa

rabbit

waabooz

wapos

buffalo

mashkodebizhiki

<u>paskwawimistos</u>

duck

zhiishiib

<u>sisip</u>

moose

mooz

moswa

loon

maang

mwakwa

beaver

amik

amisk

muskrat

wazhashz

wacask

otter

nigig

nikik

elk

omashkooz

wawaskesiw

goose

nika

niska

turtle

miskwaadesi

mikinakos

bald eagle

migizi

<u>mikisiw</u>

fish

giigoo

kinosew

caribou

adik

<u>atik</u>